Seer's Guidebook

Enlightening Thoughts Vol. 7

By Ron Bracale

Introduction

Seeing does not refer to looking with the physical eyes, nor perceiving with the material senses, but rather is the art of perceiving with the mind's eye. Seeing can trigger visual, auditory, olfactory, or other inner perceptions as the human form translates the impressions to make them more accessible, but these are secondary effects. Seeing is a knowing without thinking and is a wisdom which can only be hinted at by poetic, lyrical dialog. Seeing is an innate natural ability of the human form which must be cultivated in order for one to have awareness of this faculty. It is not intellectual, nor does it require a specific belief system: it is experiential direct perception.

Living in the Seer's Way is a calling. It is work and yet it is play; and also effortless activity, as well as stillness. To use words is paradoxical, but so is the journey of Consciousness. It comes when one finds an inner peace that is known by being your true self, fully alive and loving. It is a balanced path which cannot be found in either asceticism or excess. When one first glimpses beyond the veil to perceive the glorious luminous foundation it should not be conceived of as attaining enlightenment. True enlightenment is a verb: actively being a loving person.

To become a Seer is to connect with nature, with one's true self, and the living Earth. There is no greater awe inspiring beauty than to perceive the active luminous web of the superstrings of our relationship with the natural environment. A Seer settles in deep peace and centers in pure luminous Consciousness and then experientially shifts and the realm of light overlays the shadow realm of ordinary existence. Only in the silent and receptive center of being can the shift be experienced. It has been referred to as second sight, but it engages a faculty beyond the senses and then the human form engages the senses and one has the vision, or hears the divine music, or feels the breath of spirited mystery. Seeing is an active, dynamic art of receiving communication from the natural realm of the Sentient Mystery, the totality flowing in the Way.

Gender Neutrality

We use the pronouns 'I' and 'You' as Gender Neutral designations. We combined Mrs. and Miss. to Ms. in order to remove a designation which only applied to females and simplified the situation of referring to females which we did not know the marital status of. In this text I use E to replace 'He / Him / She / Her' and E's to refer to 'His / Hers', thus eliminating any gender bias. I believe that in professional environments this solution would simplify many situations, as well as contributing to gender equality. This poetic teaching is equally applicable to any gender identification which the reader may have.

This teaching is about becoming totally human, which is divine, rather than becoming an imagined divine nature that is something else, or something elsewhere, which is not human. If a person is to learn to See, E must become E's true self. Everyone has a personal gender identification and no two people are the same. We are all unique and that uniqueness should not be limited by stereotypical roles. Humans are a spectrum and the duality 'either or' is an illusion. In learning to See, you will See yourself. To have peace, you will need to be a true expression of your unique loving nature.

About the Author

In many ways I am a humble, ordinary human being. My farts stink just like yours do. I make no claim to being a super-being. My youth was traumatic by the very nature of being born is a lost pre-civilized society and realizing that humans were by nature lost creatures, disconnected from nature and their true meaning and purpose. Through intense seeking to find myself I came to the realization that I really needed to just be myself. I sensed that the meaning of life was in the action of living life, rather than a mentally attained definition of life's meaning.

I devote myself to meditation, not as a sleepy escape, but rather as a passionate experience of being. I work to be meditative in all my activity, as well as in my quiet times. At one point early in life I glimpsed a deeper reality upon which the reality I had previously known was embedded in and which the mental illusion of philosophical materialism was obscuring. It is this clear view which I seek to share in this poetic narrative.

Linear thinking cannot grasp the essence, but the essence can be experienced, and so my gift is to set forth these words in hopes that the experiences of your life bring you new awareness and reading this may help you to fulfill your life purpose. Your purpose is as unique as your life experiences. The current paradigm of material reality does not encompass the Consciousness of life and the Mystery of the order of the Universe as a verb. There is much more than our senses have been trained to focus on and there are many subtle experiences which we have been trained to filter out. There is a vast array of new experiential levels which are possible for the human form.

Humanity's conditioned limitations are not some grand conspiracy, but rather humanity is continually in the process of growth and few have been explorers into these as yet unknown realms of perception. Just as a child does not know many things, humanity is in great need to wake up and experience the divine nature of experiencing the multidimensional nature of life.

Many who are reading these words understand this truth, but please contemplate these words deeply, for they may provide you with new insight into the 'Art of Seeing'. The Art of Seeing is not symbolic, nor intellectual, but a set of perceptions which can be directly experienced by the human form. Seeing is an art which will take humanity many millennia to perfect, but the time is now for all humans to break the spell of the religion of philosophical materialism and begin to learn.

Art

This manuscript is a work of Art. As Art, there is a feeling which is the essence of this work. Please transcend linear thinking and embrace cyclic poetic expression as you experience these thoughts of mine. Capture the wonder and glory of the majestic mystery of life as a journey and of the Universe as a verb. These words are meditations which I am sharing, motivated by my love.

Contents

Meet the Seer

Luminous bundles
Assembling Consciousness
Eyes touching the stars

Three-dimensional space (length, width, and height) and three-dimensional time (past, present, and future) is a world view which is embedded in a higher dimensional matrix. The Seer can glimpse beyond the boundaries of three-dimensional space-time experientially, yet putting E's direct sensing into words is by default only a symbolic and poetic representation of these experiences. The two dimensional image on a flat screen has no depth, yet when Consciousness becomes involved with the symbolic portrayal it can interpret the data as a three dimensional representation. The process of rendering a three dimensional drama from a two dimensional flat screen is similar to becoming conscious of the higher dimensional matrix of the Seer's perceptions, while viewing the three-dimensional space-time world through our materially conditioned senses.

Life exists in a higher dimensional state, but our senses render a world view of forms in the lower dimensionality of three-space and three-time. The image on a flat screen is the removal of depth and the perception of three-dimensional forms in time is the removal of the Seer's view, from which intuition and creativity descend. Human Consciousness, which is living experiential sentience, is conditioned to render life in three dimensions, but the three dimensions are not the lives being lived, just as a flat screen is not a real world that is happening. The living, perceiving Consciousness can imagine the flat screen as a world happening, but it is not. The material world view is Consciousness imagining life as limited to a three dimensional space-time bubble of body in physical world. Seeing is experientially stepping up dimensionally and feeling the greater matrix of the connectivity of natural existence.

The Seer is very functional in the substratum of three dimensional life; but E perceives the journey in a higher context. Consider a sundial and imagine that our three dimensional form is the shadow of the sundial. When the sun rises, the sundial shadow begins its existence. As the day progresses the shadow ages; first growing and then shrinking. At sunset it is again absorbed into the greater shadow of night. The sun does not cease when the day is done and the shadow becomes part of the night. The human form emerges from the higher dimensional matrix at birth, grows and ages, and then returns to the Earth. The Seer experiences the transformations of the shadow of the human form from the point of view of pure shining Consciousness.

If a sphere falls through a plane, from the plane's point of view a circle expands and contracts. This growing and shrinking circle is limited data to construct the idea of a sphere from. The thing about a shadow is that there are two aspects which create it, there is the light and there is the object which creates the shape and qualities of the shadow. Our senses have limited data and have perceived a set of boundaries or surfaces where the higher dimensions intersect to form the shadow of three dimensional space-time. In the case of a living being there is Consciousness and there is that which we are conscious of, referred to here as the Sentient Mystery. Consciousness is receptive: it perceives experience. The Sentient Mystery is active: it has a spirited nature and follows a specific Way (according to the laws of nature). The senses are extremely limited and form a world view based on their interaction, but the world view is a shadowland. It has been called an illusion, but would be better described as a very limited reflection. If one takes a photo of a person, one has an idea of a person, but a person has an inner life that is amazingly complex and has emotional and mental dimensions. A living being is an infinitely complex assemblage of ever transforming superstring waves. The Seer perceives with direct experience the higher dimensional realms of being.

The Way of the Seer is freedom. E is a real human, full of peculiarities and eccentricities. E has inner peace with personal uniqueness, such that there is no need for a false persona. E is not predictable in that E reflects the ever changing truth of the Sentient Mystery. E does not meet the expectations of others: E walks in the Way of E's personal nature. E disturbs the status-quo.

The Seer, by staying true to inherent uniqueness, wakes people up to their true nature. Waking up is unsettling; fantasies fall away and the truth of being human is realized. Humanity has the potential to be a species of Seers, of awake and loving beings who embrace the Sentient Mystery and know that the organic human form is also a divine Mystery. There is no duality in this. Being a true human is a blessing: a wonderful gift. The pain and sorrow, the pleasure and joy, and the entire infinite array of feelings stimulate the essence of Consciousness as we humans take this miraculous journey of learning to love ourselves and love others in the truth that we are together as aspects of the living Earth and the sacred biosphere. In our healing we learn that the stars beckon us to explore the endless, wondrous Sentient Mystery, both within and without. The Seer lives life honoring the divine gift of precious awareness and the sacred nature of life, the Mysterious journey we take.

Everyone has their own point of view and having the perspective of the Seer's vision is not a known option in the world view of many people, but the time is approaching when the reality of the Seer will be accepted and respected. Some may interpret these poetic words as nonsense, yet whoever pauses will recall moments in their life when an extraordinary experience (such as an intuition or synchronicity) did not fit the false religion of philosophical materialism and then these words will resonate and awaken a deeper understanding. Then with intent, by being present and watching the flow of events in time more closely, one will realize they are journeying through a Sentient Mystery. There is more that is unknown than our limited world view will ever know. All that is, is teaming with life, with Consciousness, which is flowing through a Sentient Mystery.

The Seer embraces balance: reflection and contemplation balances action, receptivity balances creativity, and perception modifies intent. Many things may be discovered and the journey one chooses potentiates the order of uncovering Mysteries. Expanding awareness to encompass more of the Mystery increases the guidance which one has available. Stillness and quickness reside together in the inner core of the Seer. In balance: the receptive energies bring power to the active energies and the active energies cultivate the receptive energies that they may blossom in their true glory. Empowerment is bringing the true nature of the receptive and the active energies within one's self into balance, such that they may complement each other and bring wholeness.

The Seer senses a time before Earth was a battleground. E holds a vision of the future where Earth holds one people at peace. Ominous omens of a great fall, where the world view of the ego fills the Earth sphere with destruction, herald a new age of peace where unified humanity fights great odds to survive. A world view of balance returns prosperity of spirit, our will to be in communion with the whole. Life is filled with struggles, growing pains, and the humbling face of death; and so the Seer embraces compassion. Once one Sees the mirage of false materialist paradigms E can no longer be deluded: the essence of Consciousness, once known, dissolves all illusions.

Healing is being healed. We are all energetically connected and so the Seer has no ill wishes for any other being. Those who are self-appointed enemies of the Seers are seen as delusional egos and E works to awaken them to their true nature. E's way is to love everyone as the self, for we are the organ of humanity within the biosphere and we must function as one unified people to be healthy, vital, and receive the gifts of prosperity. No two beings hold the same point of view, though similar points of view exist to create world views. A Seer may only help others to enhance and enlarge their own limited and limiting point of view with the intent to awaken our shared nature and bring healing.

The Seer is humble and knows their mortality. E accepts their garb of flesh that allows the journey and lessons of a lifetime. E distinguishes between conditioned desires and true passion, which is the purpose ingrained in their life journey. E differentiates conditioned aversions and fears from true omens of danger. E faces the blockages which must be bravely engaged and overcome to be the person they were meant to be. E walks a true path to death, knowing that E must live with all their choices forever.

The Seer avoids judgement. There is no good and bad, only wisdom and ignorance within the ever-changing Mystery. Wisdom is a reflection of the Way that nurtures life and Consciousness. Ignorance is any world view, illusion, or delusion which does not nurture growth. Wisdom increases inner peace, while ignorance gives rise to unsettling emotional states such as worry, anger, and fear. E does not condone actions which are not expressions of love; but has only compassion for the lost souls who guide themselves with selfishness instead of love.

A Seer is aware of what passes through the inner spaces as feelings, thoughts of the mind, and the content of dreams. E uses objective discrimination to determine what feelings to focus on and what feelings to let fade into the past. E uses objective discrimination to determine what thoughts to follow and what thoughts to let fade into the past. E has non-judgmental compassion for self and is able to settle into inner peace to receive guidance from the Sentient Mystery and to channel artistic expression in everyday life. The human form has tendencies which require strong will and clear understanding for the Seer to guide the path being chosen within the Way and attract future experiences which enhance awareness.

The Seer is a multidimensional being. A description such as 'body-mind-emotions-spirit' is extremely limiting and also adds false lines of separation within E's unified being. Expounding lists like seven chakras (physical, sexual, vital, emotional, communicative, mental, causal) may be good mental exercises, but the luminous core of a human is extremely complex. The mental view of acupuncture channels and points on the surface of the luminous bundle of superstrings hints at the complexity of a living being and yet is very incomplete.

Superstrings span the universe and wind through a living being's core. Within the human form are natural doors and powers of perception which cannot be described, but which can be experienced. Seeing is not magic; but rather, it is an inheritance: an ability within the human form which the future is calling forth into manifestation. Limiting descriptions leave out that for which there are no words to describe. Words are symbols which represent elements of experience. All experience is the indescribable interaction of Consciousness and the Sentient Mystery. This poetic narrative is adding the symbolic framework for the experience which the Seer lives within.

A Seer Sees the change in the quantum flux of the superstrings over the course of a day, the lunar cycle, and the seasons of the year. E perceives a quickly racing flow as the luminous web which connects all of life changes. E hears the music of the superstrings vibrating against each other and the symphony of the cycles of nature shifts with the time of day, the time of the moon, and the time of the year. E is aware of how the music of nature, the radiance of the sentient quantum flux, changes within and utilizes that wisdom to enhance awareness.

A Seer rests in the glow of the Earth. The biosphere exists within the dense area of the Earth's aura. This 'glow' is really countless superstrings shining with Consciousness, so fine that they are perceived as a glow. All Earth's living beings are entangled in the Earths web of superstrings. E also feels the connection to the celestial bodies that the Earth dances with. The Sun's vast flux of superstrings holds the Earth in a delicate dance. The Moon's superstrings caress the Earth with delicious cycles which ebb and flow, stimulating the luminous bodies of all living beings. The planets and the stars turn within the bundle of luminous superstrings that make up a living being. The true nature of all things is transformation and the Heavens are the time master.

The Seer perceives all living beings as microcosms reflecting the dance of the Earth and the heavens. E works with the flux within to understand the ebb and flow of awareness. Just as the luminous Consciousness shines during the day and sinks into the dark Sentient Mystery at night in dreams, one also changes with the lunar phases and the seasons. The forth cycle of ages also turns within humanity as a whole. The dance of Consciousness with the Sentient Mystery is a dance with the cycles of nature.

Seeing is the art of transcending one's personal point of view and experiencing formless perception. E maintains a formless state which is open and receptive in conjunction with a very focused and disciplined personal point of view. Attention is both focused for perception and open for reception. E's art is to join the two modes of attention and live with them simultaneously engaged. E, with the two attentions complementing each other, lives in the balance of wholeness symbolized by the circle.

In the Seer's experience Consciousness is the sentient cloud of superstrings that are woven together and upon which the human body rests in an extremely complex and dynamic flow, but the overall basis is balance, harmony, and resonance. The elements of balance are health and life. The glow of life is the hum of the superstrings in the intricately woven form of a living being, interacting and playing the symphony of a life stream. The aura is trillions of sentient fibers, fluid rays of perception's light of Consciousness connecting one to all other luminous clusters of superstrings in a glorious web of life. It is this living higher dimensional experience of the Seer which is diminished into the three dimensional space and three dimensional time world view of philosophical materialism, a very sad and limited world view.

Light and Dark

bright Light – dark Shadows
more is Hidden than Revealed
Living Mystery

The Seer refers to the Sentient Mystery as shadow and darkness because it is hidden and unknown to the mind. The Sentient Mystery contains vastness which the light of Consciousness has not yet illuminated. What is unknown is invisible. Shadows provide depth to that which the light illuminates. The Seer knows that within every person are talents and potentials that are waiting in the darkness of the not yet known. E radiates a presence and those vibrations touch the strings of potential in the darkness of others, causing those hidden talents and potentials to resonate and come into the person's own light of Consciousness. In the shadows of others, Seers become aware of the shadows within themselves, to continually grow into new potentials. The Seer's art is to actively delve into the shadows of the Sentient Mystery, to shine the light of Consciousness into the unknown and to glimpse the magic of the unfolding mysterious journey of life.

The Seer journeys through the light and the dark in cycles and embraces both experiences equally. E cultivates inner life as diligently as managing the outer life journey in the world. E accumulates inner treasures of being and uses these assets in the outer journey where the richness of relationships and loving energy are enhanced. Material riches may come and go while the Seer accumulates the powers of Consciousness. Through receptivity of the Sentient Mystery which weaves the journey, E lives in the present with creativity: fully alive and aware. E follows synchronicities throughout the magical journey of the light and the dark of a mortal lifetime.

The future is obscured and dark, one's light cannot illuminate the shrouded multiverse of potentials, but cloudy visions fill a Seer with intuition and E reacts with spontaneous agility. The webs people weave all get undone, while nature progresses through continual renewal. A Seer sends out ripples without attachment, knowing that nothing can be held on to as the fields of manifestation are in continual transformation. E watches the shadows because they hint at the unseen which is giving them form. E reads and follows the signs along the journey without the possessiveness of a specific imagined destination.

The Seer is steady amid both exhilarating situations and amid dismal repetitive monotony and maintains connections beyond the present illusion of three-space-time. E distinguishes between imagined fantasy and the whispering of the omens of the spirit of the Sentient Mystery which tells the fantastic story of birth, the entering of Consciousness into a time tunnel, life's transformations, and death's release into the openness of communion with the essence of Mystery.

The Mystery is Sentient: the Seer is in relationship to other living beings and the unified web of the biosphere. The Sentient Mystery holds Consciousness within its many diverse forms and casts transformative conditions to lead Consciousness on a journey of discovery and awakening to ever greater awareness. Every bundle of Consciousness is wrapped in the Sentient Mystery's arms and The Sentient Mystery delivers intensifying experiences which promote growth. All form will be dissolved and all that is witnessed melts into the past; however, the Seer is one who has realized that E is the Consciousness and not the journey: not the body, mind, and world forms which are aspects of the journey.

The past is not a linear story. Every person who lives has a unique history and perspective. This means that the past is multi-dimensional containing time lines with every thought, feeling, and higher dimension aspect of perception which has been experienced. Every culture and sub-culture has its own history and world view of unfolding events which is a story of the past, but not the past itself. The Seer knows the illusion of linear history or any view of the past which is cast as a story. E has undone all personal stories of E's past and been released from the binding influence of personal stories. E has realized their past as a mysterious journey. People hold onto specific events and weave them into their personal history, ignoring or forgetting countless others. E has released the focus on specific events and thus freed E's present to be a free dance in the Sentient Mystery. E is not a defined personality, but is a growing and evolving being. E has no mental constraint or belief resisting truth and so E is free to make the most loving choices in every present situation.

The Seer holds the keys of many future potentials. E shares some keys and hides the rest in artistic abstraction. E has vast power which is tempered by love and expressed through patience and gentleness. Once a truth is revealed, seen, and known; it cannot be unknown. The truth can be shattering to those who are embedded in false world views and E is compassionate. Knowledge is power and a Seer does not share knowledge with those too immature to wield the power with love. E is compassionate and teaches the Way through radiating it. Only in the Way may life prosper. Flowers fade, but leave behind seeds which are the keys that allow more flowers to bloom.

A Seer is aware that the Sentient Mystery is aware of all that passes within the mind and therefore E watches for the Synchronicities that provide clear guidance. The Sentient Mystery knows every person better than they know themselves. The Sentient Mystery is subtle in the alignment of time lines such that each person is challenged to become more self-aware and grow into a more conscious being. The Sentient Mystery respects individual's free will and personal choices, but continually adjusts what is flowing down from the future into the present with new lessons and opportunities to grow and manifest an individual's true, unique potential. The shining light of Consciousness is continually refined by the dark Sentient Mystery.

A Seer does not have a static sense of self. E is a morphing being, forever growing in awareness and adopting to the flowing Way of the Sentient Mystery. E's world view contains no nouns, for all things are temporary and continually changing verbs. E is a guest of the Sentient Mystery, a visiting journeyer. Each moment of life, each breath, is an amazing adventure, a miracle to behold, and an opportunity to experience the Sentient Mystery more fully. E is the essence, the Consciousness that illuminates, engaged in a dance with the dark and mysterious spirited order threading through the transformations of form. E is illuminating the darkness through the experiences of the miracle of life and love.

A Seer is both bright Consciousness and dark Mystery. E's body is a servant. E's mind is a servant. E's servants are the Seer's advisors. The servants do their jobs and bring awareness to the essence. Consciousness is like a wind which causes glowing perceptions to illuminate different parts of the vast weave of superstrings that are the living totality. It is like blowing on a fire where the kindling is not consumed, but which has many fibers which flame up and illuminate the darkness. Consciousness is a non-local fluid wind and like the wind it is invisible and yet it touches form and illuminates form. Form is the clothing of the dark Sentient Mystery which is ever changing in spirited transformations. Consciousness and the Sentient Mystery empower each other as they dance.

The Seer delves into the secrets embedded in the shadows of the Sentient Mystery. The Seer's Consciousness follows trails though the mystery, uncovering and bringing to the light the relevant aspects which promote growth to the next level of awareness. From the endless realms of the Sentient Mystery, the future has threads which can be followed by the human form and the Seer perceives those time streams and E feels for the ones which will enhance the essence of Consciousness. E cultivates a relationship with those time streams with the intent of engaging deep experiences of those aspects of the Sentient Mystery. E is enamored with the dark unknown potential and touches and feels for the threads which will bring down the magic of life from the future multiverse of possibilities.

The Seer weaves a web, intricate and beautiful, with intent according to E's nature. E weaves a web of sentient luminous superstrings, choosing and rejecting fibers to spin around and through E's life stream. E toils through the night and sometimes the webs collect dew, like precious pearls which glitter in the sunshine of Consciousness and like the stars shining in the infinity of vastness. E's art is mystery interspersed with lenses which reveal the intertwined soul lights glittering from within the darkness of form.

The Seer faces the unknown: the divine Mystery pulsing with cyclic energetic exchanges. E's luminous Consciousness shines into the dark unknown which is woven with spirited order by super-sentient Consciousness in hierarchical ascending layers of being. E is disciplined and control's intent with love in service to the super-sentient living river shrouded in the deep dark Mystery. E is the Conscious light having direct experience within the dark, unknowable hidden folds of the spirited order of life's journey. E's quest is to brighten and expand awareness through the Sentient Mystery's weaving of the living time lines interacting with E's journey.

The Seer potentiates creativity through receptivity. True creativity changes the paradigm by which the mind conceives reality. The Sentient Mystery is beyond the paradigm of space and time. The Sentient Mystery can be experienced through pure receptivity. The Seer is in contact and communication with the Sentient Mystery. E knows that every living being is a Sentient Mystery, an aspect of the divine, from which Consciousness shines. A living being is a shadow which reveals the light of Consciousness by its existence. The shadow only exists because the light of Consciousness is visiting. When the light moves on, the shadow form returns to the darkness of the Sentient Mystery, the totality in which all form dances in the Way.

The art of the Seer is to maintain center as the radiant light of Consciousness, even amid chaotic situations or transitions. The shadow of form is forever transforming and all situations, events, and conditions rise and fall amidst an intricate weaving of the Sentient Mystery's teachings. It is not given for moral life forms to understand the vast and complex totality of which they are a part, but the visiting Consciousness experiences and interacts and is thereby slowly intensified.

A tree is a magnificent being. If one encounters a tree from consensual reality, the descriptions of the world view get applied, even though one might gaze at it and feel wonder and glory. A Seer perceives the luminous glory of the living being in the tree body. A Seer knows that at dawn light fills leaves like unfocused multifaceted eyes and a being perceives and experiences life. The Seer can commune with the tree being. The art of Seeing requires inner peace: no words, no description, and no layers of preconceived ideas – just direct perception, present experience. A tree is a bright luminous Consciousness and a dark ordered mystery.

The light dances with shadows. The darkness is infinitely vast and only minimally penetrated with the light. Shade is delicious and sunshine is delightful. The dark and mysterious holds endless hidden treasures for the light to shine upon.

Seer's Understanding

A Seer uses compassion and mercy as the basis for personal growth. E is gentle with inner darkness and nurtures the radiance of awareness. E patiently audits E's inner baggage and gradually casts out the thoughts which do not support refinement. Seeing oneself truthfully can be a harsh reality. E does not torment their mind, nor feel sorry for their lot; as such activities drain one's energy. All situations pass into history. All situations can serve a purpose for growth and refinement of awareness. All emotional baggage clouds the clear light which must discern the loving path. Mortal life is humbling and the Seer is accepting, yet E is able to creatively expand Consciousness in all situations. E struggles like all mortals and yet has an inner peace which allows a higher dimensional view. E knows death stalks and yet is not filled with fear at the inevitable. E is inwardly merciful. E does not focus on what could have been if fate had been different or what life could have been like if E had made different choices, as these activities are stealing energy from living in the present and fulfilling what the moment can be.

A Seer does not seek to influence others. A Seer radiates vibrant superstrings with loving life force, which naturally attracts people to the Way without enticements. Impinging upon another person's energy body with physical, emotional, or mental intent to influence or manipulate them causes distortions in one's own energy field and drains one's energy such that one cannot See. Seeing requires freedom. Only through consensual interactions may one's energy body remain complete such that one may See.

An empty and open mind has space to receive, if the

emptiness and silence is filled with a quick listener. Seers embrace conscious intensity in present experience: fully alive and receptive to the sensory steams where the complex weavings communicate wisdom from the living mystery of the Universe indicating life's optimum choices. The design of nature holds ancient wisdom and timeless truths: The human form inherits the ancient wisdom and timeless truths. Balancing inner and outer which are intimately connected reveals the indescribable nature as a conscious experience. Humans are cells in the Earth's body: Humanity is an organ system in the Earth's body; an organ system with the function to be stewards of the biosphere. Seers are healers empowering the life force, the source of natural creativity which manifests in spirals of ever more conscious life.

Nature has some inflexible rules, sneak around one and nature will appear with swift realignment, returning things to the Way. The Seer reflects on personal actions, not for self-judgement, but for self-refinement: forever growing in self-awareness. Knowing the Way is like climbing a mountain where each step is a choice which reveals the next potential steps which are available to choose from. Some choices lead to dead ends and sometimes backtracking is required to find the Way. As clarity comes and the landscape is learned over a lifetime, the Way is revealed.

The universe is filled with life. There are many unseen dimensions: from the atomic, sub-atomic, and quantum realms to countless unique galaxies filled with worlds that are filled with life, and yet this is the five percent, while the hidden dark plasma and the bright energy are just as complex and filled to the brim with intricately layered mysteries. The universe is spirited and filled with an order which is referred to as the Sentient Mystery. The mind cannot conceive, but the Seer can experience and know much more than words can define.

Humans have deeply rooted world views, which are mythology and are delusions when they are confused with reality, the

Sentient Mystery. A paradigm of the world is necessary to function within the mystical dream of waking life. Luminous spider-webs of flowing superstrings entwine all living beings within the one Sentient Mystery. The body is a container, but it is not a set of boundaries. When the eyes behold a star, one's Consciousness extends with luminous sentient superstrings and connects with the star. Whatever is within one's perception, is within one's Consciousness; and therefore, is within one's self. Even the mind's imaginings and conceptions of perceived reality are internal experience: resting within one's Consciousness.

The Sentient Mystery, the spirited multidimensional Universe (not the philosophical material universe), knows us better than we know ourselves. Consciousness is where the feelings and perceptions, the experience, resides. The feelings of my hand touching something happen where my hand experiences the sensations. Though my mind happens in my head and analyses, interprets, and integrates the experience; only the experience of the thinking mind is in my head. The experience of my hand touching is where my hand is and therefore, my Consciousness is extended to the place of the touch.

The Seer resolves duality into the wholeness symbolized by the circle. E experiences the unity of diversity. Humanity, as global community, is supreme empowerment. Individuals competing against each other are a betrayal of human nature and the basis of a cultural sickness and death. Only as loving beings can humanity survive and prosper. By being aware of the whole and engaging in the relationships to the totality, the Seer transcends fear and with deep inner peace radiates love. Vulnerability is an illusion on a journey in relationship with and returning to the Sentient Mystery. Control is a delusion as the Sentient Mystery is continuously manifesting the new. Situations which are continually falling out of the future multiverse and into the present instant of the journey hold synchronistic keys for the enhancement of awareness of the interconnections of love.

A Seer understands that being relies on nonbeing for definition, yet Consciousness is and there is no awareness of unconsciousness, only a concept in the mind based upon linear time. Humans experience through relationship with space-time, yet space-time is fabricated by the mind, not the senses. The perceived human world is but one of infinite subsets of the Divine Sacred Mystery which Consciousness interacts with. Seeing is opening to a deeper connection of Consciousness with Consciousness. The experience of Seeing is as unique as the Seer. In Seeing it is a feeling and knowing where Consciousness transcends the boundaries of the world view and the self expands to incorporate the seen. In Seeing the mental concept of the Seer and the seen is gone and there is a direct experience of unity. There is pure experience without filters of definition or analysis. Being and nonbeing are absorbed in the Sentient Mystery.

The Seer has a sharp clear mind which is continually cultivated to cut through illusions and seek the truth. E knows there is no end to the illusion and more subtle layers are continually revealed as deeper truths are known. The total truth is deeper and more complex than the mind can know, yet the mind must be sharpened to symbolically represent order in higher and higher degrees. The Seer's art is to suspend the mind and completely immerse in experience and be totally present without filters to catch the essence: the webs of superstring connections and the intricate relationships which transcend the apparent. E then reengages the powerful servant of mental faculty to understand and make choices.

Seers understand that they cannot mentally comprehend everything about a situation and so they listen to spirited guidance from the Sentient Mystery to grasp the most essential elements. E feels the course of action which they are meant to take. E understands that the Divine Mystery can introduce new factors at any time; changing the dynamic and the result. E controls their personal actions and the energy they radiate, but understands that they cannot control the future. E places intent for outcomes according to the present understanding, but is fluid and shifts with time. E does not have attachment to a static view of outcomes and acts dynamically as the present changes.

The Seer understands that the Sentient Mystery entices the light to brighten. Endless hidden wonders wait within the Sentient Mystery and create a powerful desire to know, which drives E to experience life more fully. E dances with the Sentient Mystery, interacting on ever deeper levels. Dancing in style; E does not anticipate the next move of the Sentient Mystery, but rather intuits the moves and dances in real time, feeling the flow in the here and now.

The Seer accepts the mortal organic body as a lower vibrational reflection and as a tool for enhancing awareness. E is ever more fully human while perceiving the superstrings of relationships from a transcendental point of view. E is centered in the source of awareness, the essence of Consciousness, in which the human form resides. Through meditation E is settled into the center of being and from the center fills the human form with radiant awareness. E is aware of every string of spirited action and intent which E is casting out, aligning the strings of intent to creatively express the wonder and miracle of life and of the Sentient Mystery which is forever flowing through E's daily life. E embraces the organic journey of the visit throughout the many phases of a lifetime.

The Way is balance. There are oscillations around the point of the center. Nature is cyclic and fluctuates in a progression that spirals. E is one who has settled into the axis, who is the Consciousness at the center, perceiving all things fluctuating around the stillness of the sentient essence. The experience of perception changes while the perceiving conscious experiencer remains untouched. A lifetime is a wave that rises and falls. There are rich experiences which stimulate one's spirit of intent at every point on the curve. The Seer has vision which transcends the point, which is the line of dancing relationships being pulled by future potentials. The spirit of the Seer is true creativity.

The future descends on us and the past falls away, descending into obscurity, but what we carry within is our theater. The memories we release and memories we enforce are our internal stage. The present experience is clouded, filtered, and obscured by what we hold within. The Seer consciously enhances the memories that serve growth. E releases all memory baggage so that every experience is new and amazing. E's awareness is free and every experience holds keys being presented by the Sentient Mystery. The journey of the Seer is a healing journey.

Seers laugh and cry, emotional waves rise and fall, but there remains a still and peaceful meditative center where perception shines with clear light and the spirit moves with invisible intent.

The Seer's Way

the Seer's Mind's Eye
touches Superstring Fibers
Living Connections

Falling down a time tunnel, being sucked into the future, minor changes in perspective allow major changes of course. Seers perceive new levels and open new windows to know more of the Sentient Mystery. We are weaving through infinite entwined timelines; guided by Omens, cast in the intricacies of synchronicities. A Seer meditates and clears inner space to receive and intuit inspiration and live in the lucid details of vivid experience. E chooses pathways to enhance awareness, expanding Consciousness to include the subtle nuances of the grand mystery sliding by the windows of perception.

The Seer avoids dissatisfaction because E has released false demands made upon the future. E does not have expectations. E has gratitude for the present conditions and does not judge the present, because E knows the present is an opportunity to refine awareness. E is present in connection with the Sentient Mystery. E is receptive of the current situation and the potential for growth in awareness which it holds.

Death erases all of life's containers. Time dissolves all form. Experience is embedded in Consciousness. The Seer perceives the sentient order of the flow of events threads through the bundle of luminous Consciousness. With will and intent the Seer chooses to pull some strings and to push others. The Sentient Mystery drops some strings from the potential future and dissolves some strings into the past. Time is like a river and most humans stand on the shore looking out, but the Seer's Consciousness is expanded to perceive upstream and downstream. E is free of the fixations of attention which create a limited world view. One cannot expand that which one believes and grasp an aspect previously unknown by being fixated in a belief system.

The Seer's art is to open pure receptivity and let the synchronicities in the river of time present new insights though following foresight and being free of the past's assumptions. The Sentient Mystery is infinitely rich and can continually give new insight without being depleted. The future pouring down into the present does not become empty, nor depleted of wonders. Time does not run out and each lifetime is a dance of timeless Consciousness with the Sacred Mystery. The Seer knows that a visit in form is but one perspective. E is formless Consciousness with the power of creativity, artfully experiencing life. As experience washes through the essence of being E lives in connection with life and radiates creative gestures of love,

The Seer is an open channel, free of the resistance which is caused by cluttered beliefs and a fixed world view which filters direct experience. E does not focus on the waves of emotions, of temporary satisfaction or dissatisfaction, but rather cultivates a feeling of traveling, of visiting life and experiencing the present changing instant to the fullest extent. E is thrilled with the extraordinary miracle of the journey.

A Seer does not hold a grudge. All is forgiven because a Seer does not pull energy from present experience to dwell on past events. When the past rises due to a situation in the present, a Seer sets it free and moves into the future. Things in the past are what they are; and so a Seer remains present in current experience. In the present is the wonder and the glory of the living Sentient Mystery of life.

The Sentient Mystery is like a river, one must eventually go with the flow. One can seek to move upstream and oppose the current by revisiting the past, but will be swept forward. One can fight the current and seek to stay still in the present state, but the present is gone and one will inevitably be pulled downstream into the future transformations which the Sentient Mystery designs for the refinement of souls. One will flow to the sea, regardless of any effort to the contrary. The Seer knows the Way and effortlessly flows in balance.

The Seer flows like water: over, under, or around obstacles blocking E's path. E remains centered with inner peace amid conflict. People vie for the Seer's power to satisfy their conditioned desires and their own imagined lack, but E perceives the pushing and pulling and reacts with conscious control according to the guidance of the spirit of the Sentient Mystery. By staying in the spirit of the Way, E heals others, moving them closer to the Way, which the Sentient Mystery continually prepares for their journey.

The Seer is a student of life, carefully observing everything: the environment, the people, the situations and how they change, to catch the true wisdom embedded by the Sentient Mystery. E seeks to never react, but to always consciously choose what action to engage in. E navigates and sail the winds of time while most humans are like leaves being blown in the whirlwind of the events surrounding them.

Seers tug on chosen threads in the multiverse of the future's possible timelines to increase their probabilistic likelihood, while remaining free of expectations. E knows that the Sentient Mystery will pull down the future with lessons to stimulate awareness and maintain the Way. The Sentient Mystery has perfect timing and impeccable design within all form which is a temporary canvas transforming artfully in a reflection of the Way. The Seer flows in the Way and E's life is an artistic expression of the Sentient Mystery.

The Seer embraces multiple traditions and cultures and therefore can transcend conditioning. E knows the richness of being an apprentice and learning from a lineage of teachers. By embracing multiple traditions E may enrich those traditions and pass on new treasures. The Sentient Mystery is the master teacher and can introduce new elements which are hovering in the future, waiting to descend into form. A living tradition is one that grows from generation to generation. A vital culture is one with healthy transformations which are guided by the Sentient Mystery in the Way. Living traditions and vital cultures honor their roots and transmit their essences to the next generation. The art of Seeing is as ancient as humanity and yet it is the rare individual who is called and who is also disciplined enough to pursue the Way and dance with the Sentient Mystery. The art of the Seer is the inheritance of everyone wearing the human form, but one must be quick enough to embrace the Way.

Humans search for something to fulfill, yet all is temporary and unsatisfying in the long run. Humans find enjoyment and pleasure, but also encounter strife and pain. What matters? The Seer enhances awareness and follows synchronicities through situations and events. At times the Seer fumbles through worldly matters, as all humans do, yet while doing so maintains an inner clarity. The worldly matters are passing drama, temporary ripples in the illusion of linear space-time. The Seer is connected to the timeless essence. This is paradoxical because the journey continues and yet there is an essence which is untouched by the journey and is the nature of being, of awareness itself. The art of Seeing is quickening timeless Consciousness and catching perceptions of the primary fabric of the Sentient Mystery upon which the boundaries perceived as the of the manifest form rest. Manifest form is commonly perceived as a world view and falsely thought to be reality. The ever transforming forms which appear to be a conditioned reality are a facade upon the infinite Sentient

Mystery. The Seer perceives richness regardless of the apparent situational conditions. E is an active part of the richness of the dance with the Sentient Mystery.

The Passion

calm Seer within
Voyage speeding past Windows
take Time to Touch Life

We are on a journey, referred to as a lifetime. We can trace our lifeline and perceive the many other lifelines which we have shared time and energy with. We are each a unique parallel universe. For all our sharing we cannot really know another's experience. The art of Seeing is the art of experiencing the feeling of another's essence, the quality of another's Consciousness, in a direct experiential way which cannot be truly captured in words, only referred to poetically.

The guide and the guided or the teacher and the apprentice are complimentary roles. One can learn from another, but ultimately must follow their own instinct and find what works for them. Everyone has a distinct calling and therefore unique pathways to fulfill their life. The Seers Guidebook may reveal potentials, but one must take the initiative to become a Seer.

A Seer is very dedicated and deliberate in expressing love through thoughts, words, and deeds. E is creative in every act of life and does not embrace dogma or rigid belief systems. E knows words and symbols are interpreted uniquely by every individual because of their perspective and mental points of view, therefore E watches the effects of words and rephrases statements to clarify their loving intent.

A Seer understands that all people live in parallel universes and every person's understanding is unique. Everyone must find their own way and yet it is through sharing that we can all find our way. Our interconnected nature holds truth. Redefining self as relationships is wisdom. A Seer directly perceives our inter-related nature within the whole. The loving light of Consciousness embraces the dark Sentient Mystery of the journey and illuminates the phenomenal ordered detail. E expresses the exquisite beauty and magnificent grandeur of the journey: continually experiencing deeper and more subtle layers of interaction with the Sentient Mystery.

A lifetime passes quickly and one must face the door of death alone. One will only know one's own choices and the experiences of one's own life's path. To become a Seer is to become transparent, letting all the false trappings, which hide the real self, fall away. A Seer does not judge or dwell in E's past. E lets E's past inform to guide E in making choices. E lives in the present with integrity and virtue which will let E be proud when revealed in the awareness of the Sentient Mystery. The community of Seers is growing. The Way of the Seer is the future of humanity.

If you choose to awaken as a Seer, don't look back, look forward. Entice and attract a future of empowerment. Draw down a future from the multiverse of possibilities where you are true to yourself and may fulfill your life. Have no expectations, for no one is in control and the future has its own designs, yet make the choices which increase your awareness and patiently possess inner peace while being amidst all circumstances. Be quick and change with the times, but not with the latest temporary fad, and maintain your integrity and your intent to awaken to your full power.

The Seer is a very alive and sensual person with respect and understanding guiding every choice. Seers know that the silver chord is a set of superstrings which connect the dreaming body to the physical body at the sexual center: Lovers are meta-entangled. Seers know their entanglements and choose them carefully. Seers have an art of working with the fibers of connectivity; strengthening some and dissolving others.

The Seer accepts that the actual future is unknowable, the present is mostly unknowable, and the past is only knowable as a murky and distorted reflection. The three dimensions of time are all infinite with mysteries untold and are unique to every timeline of life. The Seer opens the inner door and ascends to the source of the light and releases point of view to become the essence of the experience of life. E experiences the depths, the deep dark mystery of the manifestation which is perceived as a life and the world at large. The human form has an inherent tendency to perceive the living Universe as a conceptualized reality, but a Seer knows the world as a shadow between the experiencer and the experience of union with the Sacred Mystery. E is a Sentient Mystery within the Sentient Mystery.

The Seer lives by the guiding principle of love and service to the awakening: the continual process of increasing awareness. E does not have a fixed code of conduct, but addresses each situation with clear vision to see all sides to the story and by dropping any preconceived notions which do not fit the present circumstances. E cannot take sides, but rather seeks to awaken all to the common essence of life. By making everyone more conscious, the interconnections and dependent relationships are known. E knows the unity of humanity and of the biosphere of which humanity is a part. E perceives an intricately connected web of luminous superstrings meta-entangling all of life. For a Seer this is not an intellectual concept, nor a belief; for a Seer this is a direct perception, the actual experience of the present.

The Seer is a sensual being. E knows that feelings are a more refined sense than thinking. Perceiving the emotional content of a situation reveals the dynamics better than analyzing the circumstances. Both emotional and mental impressions can be unified to gain deeper understanding. Feelings are experienced and the mind recounts what has past; recalling and analyzing. The Seer has learned to suspend the mind to directly experience perceptions in a pure state, without filters. In this state of engaged meditative experience, feelings are received clearly and specific key words or phrases spontaneously arise in the mind as inspiration from the Sentient Mystery. A Seer is a master of receptivity.

The Seer knows limits and boundaries which define the human form, the container of Consciousness. E's windows peer deeply into the hidden depths of the Sentient Mystery, which reveals secrets from the shadows, which in turn embrace E with intensity. Time lines wind around each other and the thin places allow Consciousness to mingle. Self and other are constructs of the mind and in pure interaction without filters the experiencer and the experienced are one. The sentient superstrings of connection flow both ways and the dancing relationship of Consciousness and the Sentient Mystery is a unified dance. The boundaries are porous and the limits are dimensionally transcended. The Seer and the seen, the Sentient Mystery, embrace. In pure experience the sense of separation is suspended and union is known.

Limits and boundaries shift and transform as awareness grows. The shadows of the mystery dance with the living light of Consciousness: forever enticing the Seer to experientially explore the unknown and unravel the never ending secrets. Unraveling the never ending secrets of the Sentient Mystery provides the Seer with an ecstatic journey. Pleasure and pain are passing waves amid the inner peace of a life well lived, a life guided by love. The Sentient Mystery whispers synchronistic magic which invites the Seer to fulfil their unique life's purpose by doing the work of the Sentient Mystery, the totality as an ever-changing spirited unity containing intricate interrelated diversity.

The Seer embraces the natural Sentient Mystery, while the

glittering of the world seems hollow and empty. E follows sub-lime paths up the mystical mountain and seeks to artistically share the glories and wonders beheld, while knowing that those who have not seen and consciously danced with the Sentient Mystery will never know the glorious ecstasy. E has compassion and seeks to share, to lead others up the mountain to catch the view, to behold the wonder, and to know the mystery. The living web is fantastic beyond description and reflects the ultimate truth of the unified whole flowing as the Way.

A Seer is passionate and is in a romantic dance with the Sentient Mystery. E's heart yearns continually from the inner chambers of being for the conscious touch of the Divine Mystery. E is thrilled with every movement of the dance with the Beloved Mystery. E's spirit fills E's mind with continuous steady intent to engage more deeply and fully. The Sentient Mystery knows the Seer more completely than E can know self. The Sentient Mystery entices E forward, guiding E with synchronicities, visions, and dreams which are transcendental and intimately personal. E is madly in love with life, beyond the apparent present; in love on a multidimensional level where Consciousness is entwined. E radiates luminous fibers of love and the Sentient Mystery gently embraces E and caresses E's life to brighten E's luminous core with ecstatic awareness.

The Seer's Art

Dreams within the dream
Running waters pass through form
Seers know the source

A Seer does most of their work in the invisible realms of the Sentient Mystery. E knows that words cannot reach people with an understanding of these realms, but the radiant love can touch them. E connects by placing E's luminous Consciousness on the superstrings between them and flooding those channels with awareness which is love. E has no agenda for others, allowing the Sentient Mystery to bring each person into the fullness of their being to express their unique life purpose. E can only support other people with love. E shares words as the Sentient Mystery provides words to be shared. E takes action and teaches, but is continuously aware that it is the love E radiates which is powerful and transformative.

A Seer knows that every soul has a calling, a set of unique gifts to draw down future potential and manifest the Sentient Mystery's Way. E perceives that every living being is a unique cluster of superstrings which align with specific aspects of the Sentient Mystery. Most humans have shut off their energetic connections and numb themselves from the empathic flux of feelings through continual internal dialog which generates internal emotions which are not connected to the present, but are false emotions. E finds clarity within and is therefore receptive and responsive to every relationship. The Sentient Mystery reveals some things and hides others, yet provides the synchronicities required for each person to fulfill their life's purpose, which is their life's passion. When one leaves this visit to Earth, one can only take the awareness and feelings from their life, thus everyone's essential purpose and passion is to love and be loved.

The Seer understands that superstrings always flow in two directions. E is balanced and feels equally good about giving and receiving. Energetically, E is free and acts through choice, knowing that the source and destination are within the divine mystery. E receives and returns breath to the air, E receives and returns water to the seas, E receives and spends solar energy, and E receives material for a body from the Earth and will return it to the Earth. E releases attachment and journeys in the ever changing Way.

The Seer is aware that Consciousness increases over time and the evolution of Consciousness is the essence of the process of the Way, the flowing Sentient Mystery. E sends forth artistic radiance through living true to E's nature. By living fully alive and aware, others are stimulated to see themselves and grow. Long after E is gone and forgotten, E's ripples of spirited life continue to quicken Consciousness. E is an aspect of the Sentient Mystery in action.

Seers are unpredictable because every instant of life is new and E's choices are based upon the present, rather than the past. E is not hesitant to engage in a new adventure which opens potential for artistically expressing the Sentient Mystery's Way. E serves growth and nurtures the new threads of opportunity to increase awareness which the future streams into the present.

The Seer respects every person's unique journey and knows that it takes many unique threads to create a beautiful tapestry. E nurtures every life-line which E encounters through unconditional loving energy. Every life thread must become pure and true for the total image of a real humanity to be revealed. E is like a mirror in which people see themselves and also see the bigger picture. By seeing these two aspects, the personal and global in relationship, people are able to find the pathways where they can live in their full potential and contribute to the greater good.

A Seer is a warrior and chooses which conflicts to engage in. Meeting force with force escalates without resolution and so E meets force with fluidity. E avoids being the source of conflict and does not become engaged unless E is inspired to enlighten the situation. No one can get under E's calm center. Words and deeds of negative energy directed at E do not cause them to become off centered. E is the source light, Consciousness, which is visiting this Sentient Mystery. Every person must make changes for themselves and must become aware of the impact of their choices, so that they can know their own reflection with all its ripples.

A Seer does not judge others. All judgements cause the blurring of a clear view. Judgements do not allow the deeper truth to be seen clearly. Within the present are echoes of the past which are embedded in layers of vibrational feelings. Within the present are the strings of future potential tugging for dominance. The present is the axis, the fulcrum, where choices steer the course. Within the present the Sentient Mystery dynamically maintains the Way. People's choices encounter situations influenced by the Sentient Mystery to guide them to awaken. The Sentient Mystery recycles lives to refresh and renew threads flowing in the river of life's Way.

A Seer is someone who has meditated deeply and has reached a state where inner peace exists in all their daily actions, thoughts, and intentions. A Seer has disassociated from the thinking mind's illusions which born of the thinking mind calling itself 'I'. The Seer has turned the light of Consciousness around and settled into the source which is Consciousness, the true being. The Seer is the awareness which experiences the passing mental activity, the thoughts and concepts. The Seer's mind has become a tool at the Seers' disposal, instead of a tyrant who has usurped the ruling power and considers itself the 'I'. Consciousness, the true essence of being, has returned to its rightful place as the master and the mind becomes a sharp and clever servant. A Seer perceives the thoughts that arise and guides them into the Way of loving service to the Sentient Mystery.

Seers accept their mortality and it is the understanding of impermanence that inspires E to live every moment fully alive and present. E neither abstains, nor indulges, in worldly things: but rather, gently finds a balance which promotes a life in the world that is wholesome, with the greatest richness of communion with the Sentient Mystery. Temporary rich experiences which take energy from the long term journey are passed by with the understanding of the nature of the visit in form. E seeks a life of growth for self and others as Consciousness within the Sentient Mystery.

The Seer is in peace in silence. E balances life activity with reflection. E is a listener; hearing the whisperings of the sacred Sentient Mystery. The course of every life leaves impressions in the silence, in the open space beyond our ordinary perceptual realm. Consciousness is a glow. Superstrings form a living bundle and E can read the silent lines though experiential feelings and intuitive knowing. The world of things is more aptly described as bundles of vibrations. Like a note in music they are formed, they transform, and they dissolve back into the Sentient Mystery, into the infinite silence in which all which appears exists. The totality is a great symphony which rests in the infinite silence.

The Seer develops a personal relationship with the Sentient Mystery through watching and following synchronicity. Every Seer has a personal symbolic language through which the Sentient Mystery communicates. It is like the signs and signals by which lovers come know each other, too subtle to be expressed, yet clear in the intimate experiencing of their shared life paths.

E accepts that reason cannot fathom the infinity which every living being is, nor the Sentient Mystery that encompasses all of life. The Sentient Mystery warns E when a change should be avoided, though sometimes a danger is an opportunity to learn and E is guided to embrace it. E accepts mortality and so there is not the fear of death, but instead an intense passion to live, to spread love, and to raise the Consciousness of humanity.

The Seer is a peacemaker by nature, yet is a warrior when the Sentient Mystery calls for action to serve the Way. E has no need to forgive, because E does not judge, so there is nothing to forgive. E's sword is truth which reveals ignorance and lies as mirages. E is compassionate and understands that the human journey includes getting lost in false world views. E facilitates awakening to real life where one is continually growing in relationship to the Sentient Mystery. The human mind cannot symbolize an ultimate truth, answer, meaning to life, or world view; but, a human can experience love and feel the reason for the journey.

A Seer's Humbleness

wanting and needing
the Universe is laughing
touch the Mystery

A Seer loves life. E loves nature and people; and knows people are aspects of nature. E acts as a mirror to assist people with loving themselves as they really are beneath the many layers of false facade. People live in the story of themselves, a fabricated world view that obscures their magic of being an active part of the Sentient Mystery.

A Seer admits to being wrong upon finding a new level of truth. E's life is continual refinement. Seeing is pure experiential perception and then E walks down the paths of life's journey in the human form. E is both the organic shadow and the mystical shining Consciousness illuminating it. The organic shadow is alive and within the transforming patterns it holds the supreme mystery of the journey which nurtures Consciousness.

A Seer can be lied to, deceived, and cheated. E can be murdered. E is aware that something is amiss, but sometimes accepts the path of doom, playing the part that the spirit of the Sentient Mystery has indicated. E follows synchronicity and omens rather than society's conventions.

Life will have its way with one's mortal persona, with one's form. The essence of Consciousness which observes is not affected. E is pure being amidst the doings of ever-changing form.

The transformations, the nature of the dance and the interactions of the countless cyclic iterations, are guided by the ordering intent of the Sacred Mystery. E refines personal intent and perceives the Sentient Mystery which pervades the future we are falling into. E's intent strengthens some future possibilities and releases others within the natural flow. E surfs with balance down the corridors of time. E is both noble and humble, as the mortal journey has its way with all form, recycling and renewing the Way.

Seers are vulnerable because their true beliefs are exposed and yet E does not feel the need to justify or clarify for those who do not have the experience to understand. E directly perceives the luminous glow of life and the intricate connections of Consciousness. Putting any experience into words creates a poor reflection. Seeing is even more difficult because it is beyond any one sensory channel.

The Seer does not fall in with the crowd. E does not follow the trends of the time, nor accept the conditioning of the current culture which is imposed upon the people. E does not fit in, but walks the unique and natural path of the Sentient Mystery's design which brings in a more loving future for humanity. E has inner peace with no concern for level of acceptance or popularity. E is the mirror of the Sentient Mystery and radiates with its all attractive power, which some are drawn to follow and some seek to avoid because of their insatiable desires.

A Seer carries the burden of being connected to the world of lost souls. E feels the fear and pain within the human condition. E knows that every person has their unique relationship with the Sentient Mystery. Through being conscious of the quantum meta-entanglement E feels for all living beings. E is connected and feels a moral and ethical responsibility. Every action, every thought, and every step is about raising the Consciousness and increasing the amount of light through engaging the dark Sentient Mystery. From the depths of the unknown E allows a new knowledge to enter into Consciousness and shares that wisdom to expand the world view and enliven the whole.

The Seer is vulnerable. E is a person who loves unconditionally and those who hold ignorance and the illusion of separation are threatened by love. Every culture must evolve or it will perish. Traditions are eventually replaced by new traditions, whether they are formally established or are the result of the people's ever changing world view. As the paradigm of reality evolves: so must culture and traditions. E is on the present edge of change. The energy E radiates ripples through society and the effects take time to manifest, but the tide of love is the Way and will eventually dominate. Seers stay true to love, even in adversity.

A Seer does not feel the need to correct all the wrongs of the world because the Sentient Universe will erase forms as appropriate. E feels the wrongs and is touched deeply, yet maintains connection to the center which is beyond space and time; and from there E radiates love. The Sentient Universe might seem cold and uncaring to those in the mortal condition, but it attends to the brightening of Consciousness, not the temporary concerns of the mortal condition. The present seems real, yet is embedded in higher dimensional space and the direct perception of E's view transcends the limitations of the ever changing phantasm of forms. The forms are like a compressed view of the fringe boundaries of what is truly occurring. The present instant is like a prism, but the light is before it in what is considered the multiverse of the future and the light is a beam behind it in what is considered the past, but the light is a beam continuous.

The Seer is free from personal identity and will embrace fluidity to follow the movements of the Divine Mystery. E is thoughtful, considerate, and compassionate, yet makes no excuses for choosing that which makes Consciousness shine brighter. E is also Divine Mystery and serves the role of brightening other's awareness. E's personality is natural, but it is not fixed. E's identity is fluid and every change in life is experienced with a child's eyes of wonder. E has control and discipline, but chooses Spirited Mystery over conventional logic. E remains free to follow the passion which the Sentient Mystery inspires. E is powerful enough to recognize desires and conditioned life paths as leading to illusions, as opposed to divine passion which fills the essence of Consciousness with vital spirited life force. E is free to choose that which enlivens.

The Seer's way is freedom. E is not manipulated, nor does E manipulate others. E has natural relationships. E is not a victim, nor a victimizer. E engages in fair exchange. E's way is a humble prosperity and a relationally rich life. E replaces entanglements with entwinements. The conscious loving flow of meaningful interactions and communications is one of E's treasures. E is fully human and in being human and not seeking to be what E is not, E is free. There is a divine aspect to the human form when it is fully embraced and embodied. As a human with integrity E chooses entwinement to experience the richest textures of life within the Sentient Mystery.

The Seer drinks in the nectar of life energy. E is not indulgent, not because of some code of behavior, but because to experience life fully, dancing with the Sentient Universe, E must be free of limiting burdens. Indulgence dulls awareness, while sipping the sacred nectar of life stimulates awareness. E uses discretion, sorting options and choosing those that enliven. To be full and rich in the treasures of the Sentient Mystery, E embraces the wonders of life with a gentle touch, full appreciation, and gratitude. E opens the gateway of the Sentient Mystery and perceives the luminous glory that all form rests within.

The Seer maintains an inner sense of integrity, not according to convention or external expectation, but according to inner knowing. E is passionate for truth, not fabricated reality or imagined mythology; but for the essence as presented by the Sentient Mystery. E watches and learns by removing the filters of conditioned learning to grasp new wisdom. E listens to the intuitive whisperings and follows the many instances of guidance without concern for the outcome or purpose of random acts of compassion and love. These acts were inspired by the Sentient Mystery and so only appear random or unplanned, but serve the Mysterious purpose of the Way. E follows the guidance of the Sentient Mystery and maintains an inner integrity of acting in a loving manner.

The Way is Love

Winds of power dance around the Seer. E senses the dark, invisible currents and occasionally, with great discretion, uses the light of Consciousness to pull or push at a cluster of them. In the tangled web every action causes ripples in other aspects of the web and has personal consequences. The keenest second site and the most delicate of intentions are required to balance the raging currents and sail in the Way. Every mundane action in life must be executed with grace and dignity. Every word uttered must be sent with healing intent. Every thought must be sorted and either discarded or built upon. Circular and repeating thought loops must be broken because they are useless expenditures of energy which drain the power to See. Through these continual refinements of energy one is able to receive the Seer's view. By mastering the apparent, the dark invisible realms become accessible and E's true work is engaged in. E radiates love and love is healing.

A Seer is not a hermit, yet has peace being solitary in an endeavor. E works well with people, preserving inner peace amid activity. E is never alone, because E is connected to the totality, the Sentient Mystery. The way life flows and the way pieces come tumbling down from the future to be integrated into the puzzle are an ever engaging adventure. E perceives the connections and follows the pathways presented by the Sentient Mystery. Pleasure and pain, good times and hard times cycle and pass away, but E tracks the changes and finds continual empowerment of essence. Though eventually the journey of a lifetime ends, E has enriched Consciousness and fortified inspired intent for the transition and continuing journey.

The world of appearances is like clothing on the divine Sentient Mystery, it hides the sacred, the luminous higher dimensions which the Seer perceives. The human mind cannot quantify, objectify, or analyze the higher dimensional realms, yet E can have direct experience. The senses are engaged because they are touched, yet the actual perception is through the essence of Consciousness. E's art is a meditational centering which allows awareness to merge with Conscious essence of being. The spirit of the Sentient Mystery bonds many luminous superstrings into a living being and the Seer, by cultivating present awareness and honing will and intent, masters the life force and opens to the experience of Seeing.

The Seer is completely enthralled and consciously absorbed in engaging the infinite unknown of the Sentient Mystery. The Sentient Mystery is within and without. At the deepest core, centered about E's Consciousness, there is intimate contact with the Divine Mystery. In the experience, the two, Consciousness and the Sentient Mystery, are one. In a totally present state there is timelessness. Consciousness is inside of everything and everything is inside of Consciousness. There is a shift of experience and experiencer and the Seer is merged with the seen in ecstatic unity. E rides the waves of superstring sentience where the connections flow as relationships within the unity. No matter the pain or drudgery of mortal existence, E has a treasure and words may only poetically hint at the existence of the greatest richness.

The spinning Earth balances upon invisible superstrings. The glorious Sun rides on invisible superstrings through the field of stars. E feels the tension and release of the cycling of the cosmic forces of the invisible realm, the dark Sentient Mystery, as those forces hold the realm of appearances in the Way. The innate nature of the ever transforming form is resting on Consciousness, the luminous realm which E perceives. Everything is inside of Consciousness.

E can guide others along the paths which E has gotten to know, even though everyone's journey is unique. E is continually washing out the mind and cleaning out the mental clutter. E has transformed the spoiled brat of the ego into a disciplined servant. E continually gathers wisdom from the Sacred Mystery, bringing it into the present and tasking the temporary ego in the temporary human form into storing the wisdom and finding ways to express it and to share it with other pilgrims who journey through their lifetime gathering awareness through experiencing the gems of the Divine Mystery.

The Seer calls to those who can hear and draws them into the comforting and encompassing embrace of the Sacred Mystery. E tenderly undresses their egos, removing the layers of conditioning in which it hides. E gently massages their egos, which are naked in the Seer's vision, and finds the areas of pain in their lives and sooths them and heals them. E reveals their true image as a reflection in the mirror of luminous energy. E perceives all the luminous superstrings which connect E to other aspects of the luminous web and gently removes those which are draining the conscious awareness. E reveals the illusions of conditioned layers which cloak the light and they dissolve like a mirage and the divine Sacred Mystery is revealed in naked splendor, glorious detail, and grand design to awaken the true lover, the luminous Consciousness of pure living essence.

The Seer remains aware amid daily activity. The heavens, with the array of stars, does not go away when the sun shines and obscures the view of them. The astral dream energy does not go away during waking life, but is merged into the obscuring view of waking life as a function which supports our spinning of an illusionary material world view. What is real is an infinite Sentient Mystery which is hidden like stars on a sunny day by our narrow focus and our filters. The Seer knows that the astral dreamer's view remains and also knows and experiences the deeper essence, the core of Consciousness, the luminous source of awareness. E knows the array of stars are always spinning overhead and E knows the Conscious essence is dancing with the Sentient Mystery. E is fully alive and is the experiencer and the experienced. Consciousness and the Sentient Mystery are entwined by nonlocal and nontemporal superstrings. All is relationships and Consciousness is a light within the dark Sentient Mystery and the Sentient Mystery is a reflection of Consciousness revealing, while being revealed.

The Seer understands that force results in counter-force and one extreme will invite the opposite extreme. E seeks the center where balance rests and action is balanced by receptivity. Rather than push with force, E pulls with love. E perceives the luminous web of life and the effects of mental and emotional vibrations which people radiate. E radiates loving vibrations. Every luminous soul is precious in the E's view. Egos die with the body. All forms are shells gifted by the Sentient Mystery to Consciousness, so that Consciousness may intensify. E has gratitude for the gift of a lifetime and is respectful, using the opportunity of life for refinement.

The Seer is a listener, the experiencer of the Sacred Mystery. E removes blockages to growth by quieting the mind and settling into inner peace. The thinking mind will cloud and filter what is seen, so it must take a break while the Seer listens to what the flow of experience is presenting. E feels when an omen provides direction and catches the clues, the synchronicities, which allow true inspiration. E can then engage a clear and sharp mind to bring forth true creativity. The new and original is channeled by the Seer from the Sentient Mystery. The journey of life is humbling for a Seer as E listens for the guidance and follows through to manifest creativity which radiates with love.

The Seer lives in gratitude rather than in the seeking mode. E is present in the realm of the Sentient Mystery. Growth and the refinement of essence are present experiences. Healing and becoming more fully human are present experiences. Seeking and the desire to transcend the human experience are distortions which block Seeing. The Seer is a completely natural being in relationship to the natural Sentient Mystery which is the underlying core life experience. The Seer enters into present being fully and then experiences Seeing: divine perception and communication with the luminous essence which shines as Consciousness moving apparent form. The glorious shining web of superstrings interacts and hums with a glowing intricate beauty.

The Seer is present, but this does not mean E is in the mental description of linear time. E is Consciousness which transcends time. Echoes of the past bubble up into Consciousness and E reads these vibrations and the lessons they hold for making choices of growth in the present. The multiverse of the future which is falling into the present and collapsing into Consciousness whispers to the Seer. Sometimes statistically probable threads in the multiverse of the future tug at the Seer and E knows. Consciousness holds connections beyond linear time through settling into inner peace of pure being. The Seer is said to be present because E is centered in the essence of Consciousness, which is not confined by linear time. Through being Consciousness, the vision of Seeing opens.

The Seer understands that it is easier to get tangled up in an energetic situation than it is to get untangled. E maintains an inner peace and does not hold onto energy that does not serve to enhance awareness. The opportunity of a mortal lifetime is short and E does not indulge in activities that drain the vitality of life. E works hard and plays vibrantly, because these activities bring an inner completeness. E seeks to live life fully, as a humble human, enjoying the richness of revelations from the Sentient Mystery. E is grateful for the Journey. One is always entangled, but E consciously deals with entanglements and does not waste energy on things beyond E's control. E accepts and learns, releasing the need to control that which is outside E's sphere of influence to the Sentient Mystery.

The Seer does not leak or spill precious energy. This means that a Seer does not get stick in loops. A Seer does not keep mentally returning to past events or the past actions of people, as these leak the energy of life away from the present. A Seer does not spill energy in emotional outbursts or any uncontrolled action. A Seer has no energy to waste on anything outside of experiencing the magnificent wonder of life and love. E cultivates inner peace and therefore can move through the present in an effortless flowing. This implies working hard with discipline in a naturalness which fits E's true nature. Meditation is the releasing of effort and acting in a present state to witness the beauty of the Sentient Mystery.

Like flower petals being cast down from the future, the Sentient Mystery casts synchronicities before all. E has clear awareness to discern the path highlighted by the flower petals and the fortitude to follow the guidance. E's path may have challenges and may be filled with hard work, but E knows the true inner peace that comes with following love's Way. The Sentient Mystery offers continual grace, perpetually adjusting one's life lessons to show the Way. The Seer cultivates awareness, gathering in sweet smelling flower petals of blessings offered in a mortal lifetime with gratitude. The Seer's life has satisfaction through the choices being made in the present, leaving the wrong steps of the past to dissolve into obscurity through continually refining love.

The Seer washes out the mind and clears away wayward thoughts to create a beautiful inner space that E's original nature may be manifest. E washes the mind of worry and fear to be agile in the present and catch the whispering of the Sentient Mystery. E washes the mind of clutter and the mental loops of obsessive pattern which spill energy so that E may be receptive of the Sentient

Mysteries guidance. E washes the mind to be clear and listen to the body and the sensual streams of impressions without filters. E honors and loves their body as a sacred temple, for it is through the body that one is blessed with the journey of a lifetime and the opportunity to be love. E disciplines their mind to be a servant and councilor accompanying the Seer as E rides the body through the lifetime journey. E is the Consciousness; and the body and mind are assets which are illuminated by Consciousness as it journeys through Sentient Mystery.

A Dragon's gold or a Tiger's pearl can be horded, but death will steal these treasures. A good meal eaten with friends soon passes into the past, but a peaceful feeling remains. E knows the illusion of accomplishment and yet strives to achieve without attachment to results. Death erases fame and fortune and even planets pass away in the fullness of time. Historical personalities are just stories which bear little resemblance to the feel of the living person which they are attached to. The Seer knows that true attainment is achieved within one's being through the cultivation of Love. E becomes more conscious, brighter with the light of awareness, through following the synchronistic guidance of the Sentient Mystery woven in the perceived Universe. E embraces the journey, rather than the goal, and being completely focused on the journey; great progress is made along the winding road which the Sentient Mystery rolls out before us.

The Seer seeks the elegant solution to understanding life and the universe which the Sentient Mystery presents. Elegance contains a simplicity which glows with beauty. Elegance has no artificial trappings, but radiates with the natural beauty of the essence. The beauty of elegance is sublime. A life balanced in the Way of the Sentient Mystery contains a graceful elegance. The actions of a Seer are elegant because they are the effortless expression of true nature. E is very hard working and yet flows effortlessly with gratitude for the blessing of a lifetime and the opportunity to enhance awareness and grow in love. E accepts the Sentient Mystery's blessings as E moves through the natural process of a lifetime with elegance.

Human and Divine

body Awareness
watch emotions ebb and flow
Seer sits in Peace

Mortal humans are we, and mortal we remain. Ascension is honoring our mortal nature and being fully human, not becoming something else. By living within Earth's cycles and integrating our Consciousness within the biosphere, humanity will awaken as Gaia. Human Consciousness as a telepathic collective can work true magic.

Seers experience the horror and terror of pre-civilized Earth and work for the healing of humanity. When one's thoughts are not creating and driving one's feelings, then one may receive feelings which are a more powerful learning tool than the thinking mind. Seers breathe and center on the center of gravity just below the navel; and listen to the gut's instincts, the empathic feelings being generated through all that is encountered on the life journey.

Desire driven emotions are false: they are like wind driving clouds that obscure the sun but provide no rain. Meditation is like a clear sky into which clouds float and the sweet healing rain descends from the heavens to the sacred Earth and nourishes life, followed by a rainbow and clear skies again.

The Seer experiences the connections where Consciousness merges with the Sentient Mystery in the experiential communion of unity suffused in Love. Receiving the divine loving feelings from the higher dimensional foundation and radiating with a loving glow is the essence of healing and provides the potentiation for growth and planetary evolution.

The luminous world view of a Seer intersects infinite fibers glowing with sentience, the superstrings bound together in countless assemblage points, the unique reference frames of the individual worlds of the countless living beings we share life with.

Collecting strings with movement and in-breath and releasing strings with movement and out-breath. Inhaling and exhaling luminous sentient fibers of energy. We Eat strings, poop strings, and sweat meta-entangled superstring. The entangled web of superstrings races through fluid reference assemblies referred to as living beings with every flicker of thought and wave of emotion.

In all our relations we also form strong entanglements. In our interactions with friends we form bonds of luminous fibers and thus form networks of interconnected superstrings. In energy work we can directly access the energetic strings and balance our webs. Some strings we need to strengthen and some strings we need to release, since all these luminous strings vibrate with spirit intent, a feeling or energetic quality, which affects our assemblage of life energy. The webs are complex and the guiding principle is Love. The goal is to become Webs of Light shining with brilliance.

We are quantum entangled to all we touch and see. Every perceived impression is a set of macro-entangled superstrings vibrating at a set of specific energy levels which pass through the assemblage of our living being. We are meta-entangled bundles of superstrings intricately woven like the vibrations of many instruments woven into a symphony. Everything within our perceptual field, the stream of all our sensory data, is vibrating and impinging upon our essence, our unique energetic vibratory spectrum. Our essence is radiating with our personal energetic vibrations through our every word, deed, and creative expression.

We are entangled with the natural world. This is more than our breath cycling through the forest and ocean greenery. This is more than the living beings we eat (whether they are all green beings or not, we absorb their life force and that which they absorbed from the Earth and Sun). We are entwined with the biospheres of the Earth. Perceiving nature, spending time in the natural matrix, has a balancing and healing effect on our being.

We dwell within our bodies for a short while. Our form, our fluid reference assembly, which is our physical, emotional, and mental body, is in constant change. Our natural condition evokes many different energies; many feelings within our perceptual bubble. From the bursting energies of youth to the attention demanding feelings of aging, we are incited to contemplate our condition and refine our essence. We are impelled toward the understanding that we are sentient energetic clusters of Consciousness and we are not the physical, emotional, and mental constructs which are forever changing within their temporary duration.

Who are we? Our body and mind at ten years old is not our body and mind at twenty years old. There is a deeper essence, a feeling more subtle than any sensory impression, which is a unique energetic vibration; which is our true being. Behind the ever-changing ego personality construct, our essential being exists with a unique spectral signature.

Language is not effective in the task of conveying that which is transcendental to form and time and yet is the natural journey. The experience of living can only be reflected in poetic, artistic, musical, and other mystical creative expressions.

Our core energy body, our being of Spirit (creative intent)

and Light (sentient Consciousness), can be intensified. Our perceptual bubble can be settled into the eternal present to transcend linear time and our radiant energy can be powerful and loving. The energies which bombard us can be transmuted and transformed to refine our living loving glow. Life forces us to grow and intensifies us to make the changes to become clear and shine with Love to achieve deep Peace.

Affirmations

Say these to yourself, as they fit your circumstance and as you feel they are appropriate, in order to empower yourself. Before one can See, one must know their true self and become complete.

I accept the Human Form!

I will not feel shame for the human form. It is an amazing organic set of transformations. It has cutting edge magical abilities. It is a temporary vessel for my shining light and my active spirit. I will listen to my human form and live in balance, so that it can serve me. I will open the doors of perception and experience human life fully with love.

I will accept my mortal needs with peace and shall enjoy my human form without asceticism or excess; living in balance as a visitor and a guest of the master teacher, the Sentient Mystery. I shall honor the human form as a sacred vessel. It is an organic garment and I will balance its needs with compassion, neither seeking to deny my human nature, nor being indulgent.

I will accept my nature and have great gratitude for the experience of the human form. I will walk this life's journey with gratitude for the privilege of this incarnation, with its joys and sorrows passing through me. I will refine my Consciousness and purify my love during my human visit.

I will live knowing that Love is the ultimate asset of a human being. I accept my role as a loving human and seek to guide all my actions with love. I will strive to be kind and gentle, compassionate and merciful, nourishing and loving toward all. I will be as compassionate and forgiving with myself as I am with others. I will radiate love to myself and to the others travelers I encounter while visiting Earth.

I will embrace cooperative relationships which allow greater progress than competitive systems. I will gently form relationships of healing. I will actively support relationships which exchange empowerment for mutual growth and the greater good. Neither striving, nor being slothful, I will energetically do that which I am called to do.

I will honor my needs and become healthy and energetic that I may do the sacred work which the Sentient Mystery presents to me synchronistically. I will have compassion on my desires and know their roots. I will gently redirect my will to my true passion; gradually realigning my life with my innate purpose. I will have peace with my mortal nature and respect the human form, such that my luminous Consciousness may dance with the Sentient Mystery.

I accept my human form humbly and yet I open myself and allow my divinity to manifest. I am pure Consciousness shining through human garb, the baggage and blessings of form. I know my inner light touches other living lights through love. I will reveal my radiant light of Consciousness and let my luminous being be free to express itself naturally.

I accept that inevitably death will end this visit and so I will live with dedication to comprehend my lessons and manifest my gifts. Death is the great equalizer, the eraser of vanity and egotistical dreams, and the eraser of all history; therefore I commit my life to perfecting my love. I accept change as renewal. Birth, life, and death are but half a cycle. The darkness can be as luscious as the light is beautiful.

I will be humble and recognize errant thoughts which are

not for the greater good, but are self-serving, and not allow them to be manifest as actions in my life. I will be courageous in defending the way of love. I will not compromise because of the judgement of lost mortals. I will follow the path of love and be at peace with my unique life's purpose.

No person is complete!

I offer no being the right to use me, to manipulate me, or to have any hidden agenda in relationship to me. I now declare that all beings who wish relationship with me must do so in a manner that is transparent (completely revealed at a conscious level) and with Loving intent.

I will consider all people my equals. I treat no being as my lesser and honor none as my greater. All beings are unique and on 'learning visits' within form. I accept myself as my own master and study the Sentient Mystery to grow. I will put forth my energetic gifts.

I will not let negative energy, negative thoughts, or negative emotions which I encounter move me from my center of inner peace and radiant love. I do not judge those who are radiating negative energy, for that negative energy is their miserable choice based on illusion. I will forgive, but I will not condone. I will boldly embrace the truth and teach it. I will humbly learn and grow. I will accept change and expect change.

I will not curse another human, but rather, I shall wish that the divine Sentient Mystery has mercy upon them and that they wake up to see their demons, that they realize they are on a course toward their own detriment and the detriment of others and find healing. I honor every soul and see the potential of every person's incarnation to honor their own soul. I do not judge souls, yet I do not accept egos and their wayward paths when they mislead the innocent.

The world wants so much from me, yet I will set appropriate boundaries. If what is asked for is not the precious gift I have to share, I will continue to be myself. I will send forth my love. Those I encounter must prove they are loving and worthy to share my time, or what the Sentient Mystery has revealed to me will remain mystery as I return.

I shall be like a mirror and reflect back at others the energy which they are sending to me, that they might see their own negativity and feel the energy they send out, return to them. I will have no malicious intent. I will not radiate negative energy. I will let negative energy bounce off me and continue to shine as a loving being.

I do not know the dark paths others have walked, or the blessings of grace others have been offered, or whether they accepted the blessings or rejected them. I will offer my teachings and blessings and know that after many lifetimes they will find their true and unique loving self and become a thread in the tapestry.

I shall not accept the energy of others who seek to lead me astray from the way of love. I will maintain my serenity through being true to myself. I feel the pain and sorrow filling the telepathic web of humanity and am incited to love and heal the shameful oppressors. I will remain true to myself and not compromise my way under the influence of others. I will separate myself from those who seek to manipulate me.

No person is the ultimate superconscious being and I accept the graceful acts of the Sacred Mystery which will bring me to the next level. I will center and shine with hyper-vigilant light to catch the messages of the Sentient Mystery which guide me though this incarnation and free me to manifest my life's purpose.

Beliefs block seeing, knowing and experiencing the truth.

Beliefs block living to our fully loving potential by overriding the feelings within. I will look at every situation without beliefs, but instead with love, to see it clearly and know my way. I will seek a vision of a bright future for humanity and I will hold and radiate the vision into the darkness until the vision manifests.

I will be successful in expanding my Consciousness to know fulfillment of this life's purpose. I will accept the prosperity of love into my life. I accept the healing of my life.

I accept my role as student and as teacher!

I shall dedicate myself to the enlightenment of humanity, which is one component of the living Earth. As an aspect of the Divine Mystery I shall radiate love, peace, forgiveness, and healing. I accept my divine potency and my divine right to express my sacred arts passionately. I accept my roles as a student of life, of the Sacred Divine Mystery, and as a teacher with connection to the essence.

All incarnate beings are entwined by the Sentient Mystery to learn lessons. I will not let others belittle my talents and gifts. I will forgive their jealousy and fears, but not tolerate energy which seeks to diminish my radiance. I shall step out of my comfort zone to help those less fortunate and less aware than I am. I will make myself available through the grace of the Sentient Mystery to transmit lessons to those whom I encounter.

Though living beings can be teachers, I look to the Sentient Mystery as my ultimate guide and teacher. I will remember my role as a student and devotee of the Sentient Mystery as I share and teach others. I will cultivate my art and enhance it by being a dreamer and visionary. I will have peace walking my road in love, not concerned with the destination, but instead being present in the journey. I will experience the Sentient Mystery with gratitude and share the wonder and beauty.

I will guide my continual transformations in the way, guided by love. I will accept my life's purpose and bring transformation to those whom I encounter through synchronicity. I will be transformed by those whom I encounter in synchronicity and love and will reciprocate the blessings.

I have wisdom which transcends words and yet shall seek to teach those caught in the illusion. I shall endeavor to break the shameful spell of philosophical materialism and heal all our relationships. I shall be a light in the dark world, as if one star in the Milky Way, doing its part to present the majestic wonder of the Sentient Mystery.

I accept the Sentient Mystery as the Master Teacher!

The Sentient Mystery, the totality of the multidimensional Universe, is the master of all masters and the teacher of all teachers. I formally call upon the sentience of the living totality and all enlightened and loving beings to teach me. I call upon the Sentient Mystery to guide my path.

With every breath I recognize the sacred nature of life and I invite the Sentient Mystery to reveal the way. I will accept the teachings of the sweet and fierce Divine Mystery as presented to me in synchronicity and situations that fall from the future. I will trust in the Sentient Mystery as the all-powerful force and will allow myself to be a servant, a tool in the hands of the Divine.

I invite the spirit of the Sentient Mystery to open the bubble of my perception and interfere with the limitations of my mind, to expand my higher senses, and lead me in service. I will peer into the dark unknown Mysteries and shine the light of my Consciousness intently to learn that which has no words, the essence of being engaged with the living totality. The Universe is the veil that thins and falls away, leaving Consciousness in naked experiential unity with the Mystery.

I will not resist the way which the Sentient Mystery puts before me. I will let the essence of my Consciousness fill my body and engage my senses to know the Sentient Mystery, within and without. I will balance my spirited intent with my Conscious light, my power with my love, and my wisdom with the Divine Mystery.

We will come closer together!

I will consciously attract those who will assist me in raising the frequency of Consciousness. I accept community with those who work to bring the balance back. I will let all the emotional baggage created by others' negative energy fall away from me and attract other love workers to assist me. I invite the spirit of the Sentient Mystery to bring together the love workers, that our journeys may be more energized, and so that we may quicken each other's growth.

I call upon the higher vibrational brings who have the intent to assist me with my life lessons to come forth in power. Make yourself known and felt. Be my defense against lower vibrational entities and free me from the bondage which they create, that I may serve as an axis for the awakening of humanity and the healing of the Earth.

I accept my free will and with my free will I invite the unconditional loving beings to assist me. With my free will I dedicate myself to unconditionally loving other beings and being an agent of healing. I will consciously mesh with divine timing, neither rushing ahead nor lagging behind the flow of the universe.

I accept my role as a humble wayfarer within the Sentient Mystery and as a bold lover of life, seeking to embody the way ever more fully. I will stay grounded to the Earth while embracing the mystery of the stars. I will share and accept the sharing of loving people.

I give permission, though the rights inherent in my free will, for the living universe to lift the veil of the illusion of philosophical materialism and reveal the naked truth of the dance of Consciousness and the Sentient Mystery which are balanced within the unity of the sacred mystical totality.

Love

cherish human form
transcendence is illusion
Love is here and now

in daily motion
stay centered in Heart felt Love
play your part given

Thankful for each Breath
Embracing our Life Lessons
Purifying Love

Beauty of the Soul
Radiant Light seen as Love
fear not, be yourself

Forgiving one's self
Love purifying Intent
accepting growing

Love's Healing Magic
Gentle with all Relations
Maintain Inner Peace

all our Family
only Love brings Inner Peace
One Humanity

Universe Humming
Melodies of Life's Rivers
Harmonize with Love

Life's Vulnerable
Fine Beauty is Delicate
Enduring with Love

*   *   *

Thank You